Henry's **H** Book

El libro **H** de Henry

WRITTEN BY **J. L. MAZZEO**
ILLUSTRATED BY **HELEN ROSS REVUTSKY**

•••• dingles & company New Jersey

First Printing

Published By dingles&company
P.O. Box 508
Sea Girt, New Jersey 08750

LIBRARY OF CONGRESS CATALOG CARD NUMBER
2005907197
ISBN
1-59646-461-5

Printed in the United States of America

My Letter Library series is based on the original concept of Judy Mazzeo Zocchi.

ART DIRECTION
Barbie Lambert & Rizco Design
DESIGN
Rizco Design
ENGLISH EDITED BY
Andrea Curley
SPANISH EDITED BY
Jerina Page
PROJECT MANAGER
Lisa Aldorasi
EDUCATIONAL CONSULTANT
Maura Ruane McKenna
PRE-PRESS BY
Pixel Graphics

EXPLORE THE LETTERS OF THE ALPHABET WITH MY LETTER LIBRARY*

Aimee's **A** Book
Bebe's **B** Book
Cassie's **C** Book
Delia's **D** Book
Emma's **E** Book
Faye's **F** Book
George's **G** Book
Henry's **H** Book
Izzy's **I** Book
Jade's **J** Book
Kelsey's **K** Book
Logan's **L** Book
Mia's **M** Book
Nate's **N** Book
Owen's **O** Book
Peter's **P** Book
Quinn's **Q** Book
Rosie's **R** Book
Sofie's **S** Book
Tad's **T** Book
Uri's **U** Book
Vera's **V** Book
Will's **W** Book
Xavia's **X** Book
Yola's **Y** Book
Zach's **Z** Book

* All titles also available in bilingual English/Spanish versions.

WEBSITE
www.dingles.com
E-MAIL
info@dingles.com

My **Letter** Library

Hh

My Letter Library leads young children through the alphabet one letter at a time. By focusing on an individual letter in each book, the series allows youngsters to identify and absorb the concept of each letter thoroughly before being introduced to the next. In addition, it invites them to look around and discover where objects beginning with the specific letter appear in their own world.

Hh

A a   B b   C c   D d   E e   F f   G g

H h   I i   J j   K k   L l   M m   N n

O o   P p   Q q   R r   S s   T t   U u

V v   W w   X x   Y y   Z z

H is for **H**enry.

Henry is
a **h**appy **h**ippopotamus.

H es para **H**enry.

Henry es un
hipopótamo feliz.

At Henry's beach hangout you will see a **h**elicopter,

En la playa de Henry, verás un **h**elicóptero,

Hh

a hard-working

hummingbird,

un colibrí muy trabajador

H h

and a happy **h**yena
sitting in the sun.

y una **h**iena contenta
sentada al sol.

Hh

By Henry's beach umbrella
you will find a **h**airbrush,

Junto a la sombrilla de playa
de Henry, encontrarás un
cepillo para el pelo,

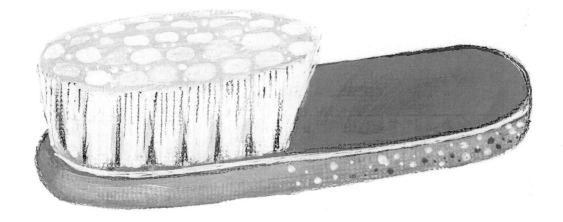

Hh

a hovering **h**ousefly,

una mosca en el aire

Hh

and a hand-held **h**armonica
for making music.

y una armónica para
hacer música.

Hh

While visiting Henry

at his hangout

you can eat a **h**ot dog,

Mientras visitas a Henry

en su playa, puedes comer

un **h**ot dog,

Hh

share a huge **h**amburger,

compartir una enorme

hamburguesa

Hh

or enjoy a **h**oneydew that Henry brought from home.

o disfrutar el melón que Henry trajo de su casa.

Hh

Things that begin with
the letter **H** are all around.

Cosas que empiezan
con la letra **H** están
por todas partes.

HELICOPTER
HELICÓPTERO

HUMMINGBIRD
COLIBRÍ

HYENA
HIENA

HAIRBRUSH
CEPILLO PARA EL PELO

HOUSEFLY
MOSCA

HARMONICA
ARMÓNICA

HOT DOG
HOT DOG

HAMBURGER
HAMBURGUESA

HONEYDEW
MELÓN

Where near Henry's beach hangout can they be found?

¿En dónde las puedes encontrar cerca de la playa de Henry?

Have an **"H"** Day!

Read "H" stories all day long.
Read books about helicopters, hummingbirds, harmonicas, hamburgers, and other **H** words. Then have the child pick out all of the words and pictures starting with the letter **H**.

Make an "H" Craft: Hip Hat
Using a single-hole puncher, punch a small hole on the right and left sides of a paper plate near the edge (at 3 and 9 o'clock).

Cut two 10-inch pieces of ribbon or yarn.

Thread the end of one piece through each hole and tape the ends to the back of the plate, leaving most of the ribbon hanging down in front.

Have the child decorate the hat any way he or she wants—for example, a Happy Hat with smiling faces, a Healthy Hat with good foods, a Hearty Hat with hearts, a Horse Hat with horse ears.

Put the hat on the child's head and tie the ribbons under the chin. He or she can wear the Hip Hat indoors or out!

Make an "H" Snack: Heart Cookies
- Use premade cookie dough.
- Roll out the dough to approximately 1 inch in thickness.
- Have the child make heart shapes in the dough using either a plastic knife or a heart-shaped cookie cutter.
- Bake the cookies according to the directions on the package.
- Once the cookies have cooled, let the child spread a thin layer of pink or white frosting on top of the cookies. Add sprinkles for an extra treat!

For additional **"H"** Day ideas and a reading list, go to www.dingles.com.

About **Letters**

Use the My Letter Library series to teach a child to identify letters and recognize the sounds they make by hearing them used and repeated in each story.

Ask:
- What letter is this book about?
- Can you name all of the **H** pictures on each page?
- Which **H** picture is your favorite? Why?
- Can you find all of the words in this book that begin with the letter **H**?

ENVIRONMENT
Discuss objects that begin with the letter **H** in the child's immediate surroundings and environment.

Use these questions to further the conversation:
- Do you live in a house? If so, what color is it?
- Have you ever spent the day at the beach like Henry? If so, did you like it?
- Which do you like better, a hamburger or a hot dog? Why?
- Look around your home and see if you can find a funny hat to wear.

OBSERVATIONS
The My Letter Library series can be used to enhance the child's imagination. Encourage the child to look around and tell you what he or she sees.

Ask:
- Is there something in your home that you can use as a pretend harmonica (for example, a comb or a rectangle-shaped wooden block)?
- Have you ever pretended you were flying around in a helicopter? If so, where did you go?
- Who did you take with you?
- Where do hippopotamuses live?
- What kinds of healthy foods do you like to eat? Name as many as you can.

TRY SOMETHING NEW...
Ask your family and friends to eat only healthy foods for one week. At the end of that week, ask them how they felt.

J. L. MAZZEO grew up in Middletown, New Jersey, as part of a close-knit Italian American family. She currently resides in Monmouth County, New Jersey, and still remains close to family members in heart and home.

HELEN ROSS REVUTSKY was born in St. Petersburg, Russia, where she received a degree in stage artistry/ design. She worked as the directing artist in Kiev's famous Governmental Puppet Theatre. Her first book, *I Can Read the Alphabet,* was published in Moscow in 1998. Helen now lives in London, where she has illustrated several children's books.